LIMITLESS

Pablo De Leon

All italicized quotations without attribution are original sayings of Pablo De Leon.

All definitions are from Dictionary.com.

Editors: Lillie Ammann and Jan McClintock

Published in Dallas, Texas, by Pablo De Leon Enterprise

First printed in the United States of America

10 9 8 7 6 5 4 3 2 1

ISBN 13: 978-0-692-38561-6

Contents

DEDICATION

After facing the biggest knockout of my life, I spent years writing this book. I had lost motivation and couldn't understand why I was losing the drive and fire I'd once had. After constant pondering, I told myself to get up and stop whining and complaining. But as filled with anger as I was, I just could not do it. I was convinced that some things had to work themselves out.

In my heart I had this need to write, but I couldn't wrap it all up, short and sweet. I wanted to give full insight into my life and my life's journey, but I couldn't do it without getting over my inner obstacles. I knew my book needed to be simple, profound, and straight to the point—not filled with anger, offering no resolution of my issues.

It just wasn't the right time for me to create a finished product.

Then I was inspired by someone who was right by my side the whole time: my brother. He was born with a heart defect and was not expected to live as long as he did. Amazingly, he never lost sight of his ambitions. And he never complained.

The trauma of losing my brother took a major toll on my family. And his passing was the push I needed to propel me to do something more than just dream about finishing this book.

I dedicate this book not only to him, but also to my family. We made drastic changes to forever alter the course of our lives—for the better. We are the Contreras family.

Thank you, Juan Contreras, my brother, for inspiring us all. You have sparked creativity in ways you never could have imagined. You have truly painted your masterpiece with the way you lived your life, and you will always live in our hearts. You are *Limitless*.

"Strength does not come from winning. Your struggles develop your strengths. When you go through hardships and decide not to surrender, that is strength."

—Arnold Schwarzenegger

FOREWORD

Knowing no fear, a lion freezes its prey with its mere presence.

As we pursue life, a part of us longs to be unleashed. Our imagination runs wild, and our hearts roar for something greater out of our lives. An actor creates and develops a specific character in his mind, bringing it to life for an audience. A batter learns to distinguish between a fastball and a change-up, gradually learning to trust his hands. A boxer wonders with every blow, "Do I have what it takes?"

In essence, these are all expressions of art. We can begin to paint our own dreams as we let the roar in our hearts be the fuel to make them a reality. Within the heart of every individual something deep within us roars, craving release.

The question is— how? How is it possible to take the negative aspects and experiences in our lives and transform them into something great and beautiful like an artist would? How can we paint a stunning future with confidence, contentment, and success in the midst of adversity? How can we overcome our obstacles so we can live a happy and peaceful life?

That is what this book is about. It's about creating a *Limitless* present.

ACTION—Prologue

"I'd rather die trying than live feeling miserably caged in."

Unleashing its power and fierce authority, a beast reacts only in accordance with its purpose. A lion roars and fights to feel like the king of the jungle. The natural way he struts with such confidence is a mystery, an unfathomable part of his powerful presence.

A lion's journey is much like a man's journey. A lion desires to unleash his power, to show his world all that he desires to be, while a man also wishes, instinctively, to fuel his purpose in life, to roam free and express himself like a lion in the wild. A man desires to live wildly and dangerously, yet some things in life tend to cage us in and make us lose sight of our ambition. Instead of acting, we only dream of being wild and beautiful. Why not try to live the dream, even though circumstances can sometimes take us in a different direction?

I don't believe that a lion ever imagines the possibility of being captured by hunters only to become a monument on a man's wall or to live in captivity, behind bars.

But, as humans, do our fears lead us to think about dire outcomes first, making us feel trapped and stagnant? Do our fears keep us so far removed from our dreams that we'll never be free?

This book describes the journey of one man's life and drive. Like a painting, it is a powerful image of how one can succeed and allow dreams to roar louder than circumstances. *Limitless* is about learning to believe again. To strut and walk with confidence, to step out of the cage of despair, to let go of the fear of failure and the fear of the perceptions of others. *Limitless* is about learning to live again.

Men and women have power that can be unleashed within their own hearts. They possess a driving force that can help them accomplish their individual purposes in life. We can dream, but living our dreams comes with a price. We have to face reality and embrace the jungles of life as we go after our dreams, never holding back in the process of fulfilling our deepest desires.

Your dreams can come true! The galaxies of possibility beyond your world live in the power of your subconscious. You are *Limitless*!

ARTISTRY

Art is the expression or application of human creative skill and imagination, typically a visual expression such as painting or sculpture. It is work produced primarily for its beauty or emotional power to be appreciated.

Most men are stimulated and motivated visually, as opposed to most women who are stimulated and motivated verbally, even though they create an image in their mind.

What I love most about the arts of acting and filmmaking is creating a visual representation of what I want the audience to see and feel using both words and images to convey meaning. This is the expression of what I hold in my heart and mind. It is my lion's roar. And it wants to come out.

Throughout this epic journey, I'll share my thoughts within these pages. I'll open up about what I see through scenes and personal experiences that I hope will inspire you. I'll show how I channeled all my pain into greatness, and how you can, too. Life is enticing and adventurous, and it's all about how you wish to create it.

Time after time, disappointment after disappointment, we develop expectations in our lives, but those expectations don't always play out the way we picture them in our minds. In fact, most never do.

I can remember having passion and desire when I was in my teens and twenties—a burning desire that could not be put out. Maybe you had that passion, too. But life beats you down and at times you feel like your dream is right around the corner but just out of reach. Years later, when you find yourself still not approaching your goal, you wonder if it's all just a fairy tale. Discouragement sets in, leaving your spirit heavy. Then comes depression.

Many never take the step of accepting the realities of making a dream come true. We have to make sacrifices to chase our dreams. The pain we encounter can sometimes cripple us along the way. Nothing feels worse than losing sight of the vision that burned so intensely in our hearts and minds.

After studying and reading books about life and evaluating what I felt in my heart, I realized I could live by modest principles and live safely or I could go for something greater with greater risk. Living dangerously and adventurously takes vision and burning desire. In order to get past the fear of failure, we have to learn that failing is not failure. Quitting is.

If you lose the fire in your heart, you have to hold on to the vision in your mind. You have to believe that somehow you will get there. This is the battlefield of the mind. I had to learn to focus less on a conscious level and more on a subconscious level, like a child who naturally acts without thinking before fear ever creeps into his or her life.

I came to this realization after several let-downs. When we try to express the things that many people don't understand or don't want to understand, we'll unavoidably hit walls that block our way. We have to recognize that, no matter what we do, even when it is the right thing, we will still have critics—and a lot of those critics will be the people closest to us.

We need to move past that, but sometimes the criticism we experience makes it hard to trust other people, especially those who criticize us while they don't live such great lives themselves. How can one person judge the dreams of another?

Who can you trust? I learned about trust from my sister, Jessica. She was born with Down syndrome, and her ability to love people unconditionally used to make me angry, both at her for being so trusting and at the people who didn't deserve her trust. I couldn't trust anyone aside from people I had formed very tight relationships with. I was not open-minded. I was closed off.

But, after a time, I realized I could no longer blame others and wallow in my bitterness, because, at the end of the day, they go on living their lives, while I'm having my pity party and dragging others down. I could no longer cage the beast that cried deep within my soul.

We all need hope and a dream to believe in. Too often we are put in a cage. Our dreams are controlled by other people who have power, who abuse their position, and who can brainwash us. We need to stop limiting ourselves.

"Dictators only believe in their own dreams and agendas and care nothing for the dreams of others."

Being controlling is another way others make sure you don't fulfill your vision. Those others may even want you to fulfill their dreams for them.

Like many families, mine was dysfunctional. My father was distant, not prone to affection. As a kid, I didn't understand that his struggles were a direct result of his own father being absent in his life.

My father desperately wanted to keep the family alive in the midst of financial struggles. Those struggles and his inability to make ends meet were devastating to his manhood. Although his frustrations manifested in an unpleasant manner during those times, today I am grateful to him for trying and for never leaving us. Watching my father aspire to his own victories and seeing the determination he had to overcome adversity greatly influenced me. He worked hard to make sure his family had more than he had.

But because of emotional abuse by extended family members in my younger years, I was filled with rage. I used to scream and yell at my three brothers and two sisters. As an adult, I decided to make an effort to improve the situation.

I went back to my family, hat in hand, and worked hard to deal with the tension in our household, to resolve our issues. My issues. This effort has since brought order and healing to all our lives. We have become a team, and since then, I've lived a better, more peaceful life.

If we can all come together, motivate and inspire one another, we can all feel and be like family.

We live in a day and age where the world needs authenticity, what I call *realness*. Pretending as though we have no struggles is not real. Churches, synagogues, or organizations that preach freedom in worship but won't allow you to be real are not helpful in the long run. One bad egg can poison the whole basket.

Be careful whom you choose to be your mentor, whether a relative, spiritual leader, friend, or colleague. You want a supportive partner when the going gets rough and the trials start to pile on.

I've been through many hardships in life and on both sides of love and hate, popularity and ostracism, wealth and poverty. I have come to learn that we live our lives more in denial than we think. Today, a lot of people live only to impress others, and impressing others costs too much! If we cannot even admit the truth about our struggles to our closest friends, to whom can we admit the truth?

And, if we cannot even talk to a so-called leader, whom can we talk to? There are those who preach a good game but never offer to lift a finger to help others. All they offer is prayer, and prayer without action is useless. I had to learn to take prayer to the next level and show with my actions what I had read about and professed to believe. I had to get real. But in order to do that, I had to un-cage my fears, bring them out into the open, and acknowledge them. Only then could I conquer them.

What's the roar that yearns in your heart and wants to come out? What are your dreams?

What fears have life's twisted punches drilled in your heart? What has made you feel like an animal afraid to come out of your cage?

"Art washes away from the soul the dust of everyday life."
— Pablo Picasso

FIGHT WITH PURPOSE

"Don't fight just to fight, but fight for a greater you."

I was not born angry, but I became a very angry young man. My parents were in the States, trying to make a life so that they could bring my siblings and me to be with them. While I was still in Mexico, I was emotionally abused by some extended family members. I kept this secret and held all my feelings inside. All that energy turned to anger, then rage. I was violently angry. I wanted to take all the violent fantasies I had in my mind and make someone pay. I wanted revenge, so I fought.

I fought in so many unproductive ways. It wasn't until I was able to come clean about my experiences that I could channel my rage. I'm still angry for that little kid, but now, I fight with purpose. I don't have to wonder why I'm fighting anymore. I don't have to question my motives. I don't have to question myself. I just have to move on and be productive.

I'll never forget a conversation with one of my coworkers. He listened to me, then he said, "Pablo, you know why I know you'll go somewhere?" I just looked at him, and he continued. "I know you'll go places because I see that you're done questioning yourself."

I told him about my second sparring session (described later). Even though I was taking punches, I kept questioning myself. Could I take it or not? Could I keep going?

I kept going. That's how life is. You've got to keep going!

I stopped questioning myself and quit making excuses as to why I couldn't accomplish something. If I had continued to second-guess myself, it would have taken much longer and been much harder to succeed. Although I—and you—will be faced with hard punches and dirty blows to the body along the way, that's what comes with taking risks.

My father always told me that life is our greatest teacher, and I agree. Life does teach us. Life gives us lessons, and I hope you can learn from them as I have. Once you learn, you can then harness your knowledge to go farther on your path to success. And once you stop questioning yourself, you might even be able to see that path as an adventure. Men and women want an adventure.

Yes! A life without adventure can lead to depression and misery. It can cause you to feel like a caged, wild animal.

Welcome to *Limitless*. Keep reading if you are looking to step out of your cage and unleash the lion within.

RESOLUTION

"Be careful how you think. Thinking positively is how you build your dreams and create your destiny, much the way you would build a character to make him or her believable. You can make your dreams come to life!"

As an artist, I have made every effort to think of my life as an adventure, although sometimes the adventures can be pretty rough.

In photography and videography, I use and hear the word *resolution* frequently. Resolution in the optical sense of the word is "the act, process, or capability of distinguishing between two separate but adjacent objects or sources of light or between two nearly equal wavelengths." Comparing things.

How do you compare your life now with what you wish your life could be?

When we look back on the journeys we've been on, our views change. And when we're challenged with obstacles along the way, we have to revise the way we look at things.

When we look at art and masterpieces that have been created, most people don't know that the best in the creative arts derives from deep challenges.

I battled through struggles I never thought I could overcome—my violence, for one, and my failures, for another. I found it hard to change my old habits. But as my mentor explained to me: A man under pressure is revealed for who he really is.

I could put on that nice, white clean baseball uniform and look like a model, but when it came time to play and the pressure was on, my performance showed whether I could deal with pressure or not. Pressure always reveals true character.

In every aspect of my life, with every challenge I face, I have trained my mind to channel those times into something beautiful. The best creations of painters or actors, singers or writers, come from their attempts to bring their perceptions of objects or light to life. That is called bringing resolution.

In production, when I want to photograph or film an object, I consider depth, angles, light, and location to give truth to the best quality of its beauty. We miss the small pieces in our lives, the little things that matter most when we focus on our imperfections rather than our best God-given qualities. Looking at ourselves through others' eyes leads to failed resolution. Why? Because the best author, artist, and writer of your life is you.

YOU!

You are the only one who can bring resolution to your life. That is, if you learn to train your mind to process darkness into light, negatives into positives.

I do understand. Keeping my own vision clear is not easy. During one period in my life, I lost total focus; my vision lacked resolution. I felt as if I were learning to operate a camera all over again. Who changed my settings? Who took my lens? Who?

Perceptions and views change when bitterness comes into play. Anger changes everything from the way you feel to the way you think. Anger also determines the many different angles by which you approach relationships.

I often listen when people tell me to have an open mind. There's nothing wrong with an open mind. Just know, however, that having an open mind can lead you to dangerous ground.

Being open to everything rather than focusing on a few goals creates risk. You can get lost. Nothing—certainly not success—is guaranteed when you are operating outside your talents.

The process of growth leads you from an open mind to choice to decisiveness to action. Don't be afraid to take risks and open your mind to the ways you can get where you want to go.

Bitterness can keep you from getting the right resolution or building the right, healthy relationships. Most importantly, though, bitterness keeps you from living a healthy life in mind and spirit.

Starting with an open mind takes discipline. Listen, observe, process. Bring the situation and your goals into a clear resolution so you can make the best decision. That, in my opinion, is having a truly open mind. Think about how your perceptions and decisions will affect you and those around you, but don't let the judgments of others cloud your mind or alter your clear resolution once you find it.

Think of what you consider to be the ugliest object, and try to find the beauty in it. Art exposes beauty that already exists. The problem is that most people perceive, judge, and act on the outer appearance of the object. They go through life trying to find their own worth and value because they cannot perceive the beauty underneath the ugliness.

Whatever objects you think about, value and worth exist in them by virtue of their mere existence. Without this intrinsic beauty, great art would not have become masterpieces.

You are that object of intrinsic beauty. Art exposes that beauty and helps you form your life into what you want it to be. And the best part is that you are the artist of your present and your future — you can make it and fashion it in any way you want. Anyone can be an inspiration! In spite of the past.

TAKE ONE—Building Character

"All dreams begin with a vision and a hungry will to achieve them."

Ever since I was a kid, I've had a passion for acting. Long before I became a baseball player in the minors and won a championship my rookie year, I was infatuated with art and created characters that existed only in my mind.

My father once told me, "One day you'll be an artist, because you just can't seem to stop drawing and coloring." I'll never forget his words.

I could never just be still. Then some folks from town drove by my house and saw my siblings and me playing baseball in the front yard. They stopped and asked my parents if we could play baseball for them.

Whatever their reality or perceptions, the rest was history. My life was taken in a whole new direction, severing my past from my future.

All my life up to that point, I had spent days and nights dreaming and creating images in my head, constantly building my world around a character I developed in my mind. Now I used that skill and, while constantly practicing and playing, I began to see myself in the pros. I created that character in my mind and I believed in him. I was driven.

Then I grew up.

What happened to that dreamy, driven kid? What happened to that passion?

My father always taught me to be observant, always aware of my surroundings without necessarily looking directly at an object. Using my senses and peripheral vision to fill in the blanks allows me to perceive many things at once.

You can explain something to me till you're blue in the face, but for me to understand and process your explanation, I have to create, from your words, a visual of what you're telling me. For me, it's almost impossible to process words without a visual. But, if you give me a visual to focus on, I will understand, which is why I love to write using visual metaphors. Talk to me, yes, but show me at the same time. Then you'll get my attention.

"You paint your life by what you create in your mind. Building a character is creating life around that character. But what makes your character come alive is believing that you are that character."

Like I created the character of the baseball player in my head, you can also create the character of who you want to be. When you are building a character in your mind, one that you want to bring to life, you have to give that character a historical background and a hint at their future.

Ask yourself:

—What are the character's dreams?
—What is their favorite meal?
—How does he or she live their life?
—How does he or she walk?
—Do they love sports?
—Do they love to travel?

These questions and others build a person in your mind. You are essentially asking yourself all the questions you can think of to figure out what the character is like and who you want him or her to be.

I was born in Mexico in an area of extreme poverty. When I was around age four, my family relocated to the United States, where I began school, although I couldn't speak English.

I was afraid of the world around me. Everything was so different and much larger than where I came from. The people looked beautiful, and I found them very intimidating. Dealing with that hugeness and that newness was a journey in itself. I had to create a character in my mind who could deal with all those changes.

I tell you this because everything I have ever accomplished in life always began with a creation in my mind and the hunger and will to achieve the goals I gave that character. Yet in the midst of all that, I always felt like the world was against me. Was that just my insecurity speaking?

Certain aspects of my life were like anyone else's life—but worse. Now I know others have had worse situations than I did, but the wounds I sustained as a youngster made it difficult for me create a better world around me. I had to go on a journey of self-discovery to get to where I am.

I seemed to have been born with a chip on my shoulder. My way of thinking always destroyed my relationships, from girlfriends to peers, coaches, and everyone in a position of leadership because of the insecure world I created in my mind and my underlying belief that everyone was out to hurt me.

Often while growing up, I felt I didn't have a gift. I didn't think that I had the real ability to play baseball. When peers told me that I had a good thing going for me, I couldn't see it, no matter how hard I tried. Insecurities never allowed me to play the game to the full capacity I intended. Fear wouldn't let me do it.

Later, when I had conquered some of my fear and insecurities, I still felt amazed when people were jealous of me, saying things like, "Oh, we can't all be like you, Pablo."

That's not true! You can all be better than me. You can be the best in areas where you are gifted that I am not. You just have to want it enough to make a few changes.

Our dreams feed our souls. Everyone has talents that can pull them out of an insecure past. Everyone has talents that can be used to reach a purpose. Everyone has skills that give them some sense of worth and value.

But first, we have to understand that we have intrinsic value, intrinsic beauty, just by virtue of existing. Once we understand our intrinsic value and recognize some of our talents, we won't have to seek affirmation of our value from outside of ourselves. We will create self-affirmation from within.

"Most of us live our whole lives without any real adventure to call our own."
—from the film *Vanilla Sky*

I came to realize that through the type of art I create in my mind, my dreams would eventually come into existence. But I had to understand the power of the formation of dreams through art. So, I began to reconstruct and recreate my life. I took all the negative things that had happened to me and used them as fuel for my dreams. There are circumstances that occur beyond our control, but how we handle them is up to us. You can let your pain keep you upset and hurt or you can use it to fuel a greater you.

Sometimes you may do things you don't want to do. However, you can use these things to help you get to a place where you are doing what you love. I went into the business of transporting petroleum. Driving a truck financed all the things I wanted to accomplish as a producer and an actor and helped me fulfill the destiny I created in my mind. I made my dreams come to life, even though I knew I could fail—and trust me, I have failed quite a bit along my journey. I just kept believing in my dreams and constructed new strategies for reaching my goals when the old ones proved not to work.

In one of my favorite scenes from the movie *Vanilla Sky*, we learn that we can glean something of value from every experience. I call this the *Vanilla Sky* moment. Every day I strive to live in the moment because I know that I am building experiences that will help me learn. And, the more I learn, the better I will be at creating strategies to get me where I want to go.

A *Vanilla Sky moment* is when you realize that every waking second provides an opportunity to turn your life around.

Every moment that we live, we have a choice to decide how to react to something. We can choose to react in a way that will make things worse, or we can choose to use the negative to support the positive. A car battery still needs the negative charge with the positive to power the engine that will take you to your destination. You need a ground wire on electrical circuits to keep you from being struck by lightning—meaning you can learn from your negative experiences and stay levelheaded enough to avoid being misled in the future.

Over the years, I have struggled with anger that, at times, I didn't know how to control. Some of you have probably experienced being told to control yourself. Even if the comment is intended to express a positive sentiment, you may not see the positive if you receive it from a different, negative perspective.

Many people make the mistake of trying to control their anger. Instead of teaching people how to control anger, we should be teaching them how to channel it in positive, productive ways.

I had to discover this for myself by reading and researching. I came across this very interesting point on anger that really enlightened me. Anger is translated from the Greek "orge" meaning violent passion that can result into a fierce rage and uncontrolled feelings of hatred. The key word is passion, which can go in either direction, negative or positive.

Do you see situations in your own life that can bring about such uncontrolled feelings of hatred? Maybe they're old wounds.

I have to admit that my anger escalated into rage because I was afraid. I lived the first twenty-five years of my life feeling like I had no control of my life—feeling that everything that made me feel inferior controlled me.

So you see, anger is no more than a passion that has been crippled by a negative perception. And passion is more aggressive when it has been crippled. But it doesn't have to be crippled forever. You can take the energy behind negative passion and channel it into something positive.

You may regard this as a secret weapon. Whether you're an implosive or explosive type of character, if you can master the art of channeling your passion, you can use that energy as fuel for achieving your dreams.

You have an advantage when you are assertively passionate versus aggressively passionate. So, if you learn to channel violent passion in a positive way, you can go far toward reaching your dreams a lot faster than most. Sitting on bitterness is wasted energy, energy you could have used to fuel you into your destiny.

Take a football player as an example. The player who hits the hardest is likely channeling violent passion. The player with violent passion will, more often than not, hit the hardest, because in my opinion, he has nothing to lose. Now that isn't always the case, because some guys are just gifted in size and great athletic abilities. Most of the time, though, guys who are smaller dominate because their passion is stronger and they have learned to channel that passion.

So we can let violent passion cripple us; we can do nothing positive and dwell on the negatives to hinder our lives from progressing. Or we can use that assertive passion to accomplish the dreams we have painted of places we'd rather be.

This transition is not easy—it is a process. To rid myself of feeling inferior to a man in a suit (because God knows I didn't grow up wearing one), I paid him a compliment instead of envying him. I channeled my negative into a positive. That's how I began to view others in a genuine, honest way because I wanted to change.

Tom Cruise's character in *Vanilla Sky* made one bad decision that cost him the dream he wanted most, but in the end he finally understood how that bad decision led him to the point of facing the one thing he feared most.

Some questions and statements that are brought up by watching *Vanilla Sky* touch on fears that keep us from living out the art of our creation:

—"What is any life without the pursuit of a dream?"

We would all die miserably in depression without the pursuit of a dream.

—"What is happiness to you?"

Go after it! You are the only one who can go after what brings you happiness. Violent passion is a driving force that can be utilized to pursue what makes you happy and to get over the bumps along the way.

—"Forget everything you know, and open your eyes."

See beyond the exterior that is visible to the naked eye; instead look deeper to where you want to be.

— "Just remember, the sweet is never as sweet without the sour."

The little things matter. There is nothing bigger. With the pain comes the learning. With the successes come the failures. I can perceive my negatives to be the little things, but they have been the fuel to make what I love become a reality.

— "Most of us live our whole lives without any real adventure to call our own."

Everyone has a story. It's what they do with it that matters.

— "I want to live a real life. I don't want to dream any longer."

I was tired of just dreaming. I wanted what I was dreaming to become a reality. I wanted the character in my mind to become believable, to be real outside of a dream. I wanted to be extraordinary. I wanted to be fearless.

FEARLESS

"Through the painful realization that the most formidable enemy lies within oneself, the martial artist strives to become a better human being. Jet's character must face the consequences of his actions. In the end, his self-discovery and the choices he made inspired a nation." — from the film *Fearless*

This is just as true for us as for the character in the movie. Rather than dwell on the negatives and continue to develop more of them, we can take those negatives and turn them into positives to become an inspiration.

Jet Li's character then goes on to become a better human being, just as we can do.

Self-discovery is a major task, and it takes a lifetime because we are always changing and always moving.

As a kid, I often thought about painting my dreams into reality. Like the *Vanilla Sky moment*, I painted a picture in my mind of what I wanted my life to be, or I played the part in a movie and created my own great ending.

Real life, however, does not always work the way we plan or paint it in our minds.

In order to fulfill our dreams, we must also accept reality. It's okay to play and paint, but when reality doesn't line up with our dreams, we can't continue to live in denial. We must accept reality so we can move on. Acceptance does not necessarily mean you are quitting. It means that rather than just daydreaming, you are taking into account the real aspects of what you have created or failed to create so you can move closer to your dream instead of further away.

For example, at age twenty-five I returned to spring training for my second season in the minors, but got injured. Because of that injury, I went into a state of depression. Even though I had originally been interested in the arts, I had come to believe that baseball was all I ever wanted to do. It was all I knew and all I had focused on.

I had no other plans and felt my whole world collapsing. Looking back at what I had done to get to the minors, I felt the sacrifices were all wasted. I was tired, with nothing to show for all the hard work.

What would I do with my life?

I had absolutely no idea. I didn't like to read and my comprehension was terrible. Even though I had completed three years of college, I considered myself too underedu-cated to do anything besides physical work.

I felt my life was over. I went back home feeling hopeless after my release from the organization.

When I returned to Dallas, I received an invitation to speak at a school. I was abso-lutely stunned by this request.

The only time I had spoken in public had been a three-minute science report in the seventh grade, which had been a nightmare I couldn't believe I'd survived. In my terror, I had been sweating and nearly passed out in front of five other students in my classroom.

How would I ever face a bigger crowd without fainting dead away?

A disaster-like scenario kept replaying in my head, but being the big-shot, egotistical guy that I was, I acted unafraid.

I accepted the challenge and asked, "When?"

The principal who invited me replied, "Tomorrow."

Outwardly keeping my composure, I said to myself, *Tomorrow? How on earth do I get ready to do this tomorrow?*

But, I had no time to let all that was happening soak in. I had to just do it. I had to face my fear.

STAGE

Tomorrow came way too soon. I was super nervous. I had no topic or even a clue as to what they wanted me to talk about. This was so sudden! I approached the principal and asked her what exactly she wanted me to talk about.

She kept it simple. "Just tell them your story."

Now as simple as that sounded, on my way to the stage, I muttered to myself, "Why in the world would anybody want to hear my story?" My hands were sweaty, and I felt like I had received a death sentence.

I knew nothing about formal introductions or icebreakers, so I had no idea how to start. Worst of all, I was speaking to kids, and kids can tell a faker from a mile away. Kids will also tell you the brutal, honest truth. They would be able to tell I was just a poser. I was in over my head, but it was too late.

So I just went straight into telling my story, despite how scared and sweaty I was. I was single-minded and spoke in simple words. Every other sentence was, "You know what I'm saying? You know what I'm saying?"

Above all, I spoke casually and transparently about my life. I couldn't believe that I saw people crying from my story. My story! Who was I? What sort of story did I have that could possibly speak to another person's heart? How could my jacked-up life have any value to others?

What sort of inspiration did I give? It's simple: IT WAS REAL. It had substance, and people could relate. I didn't have to be an intellectual to be real, and I learned later that substance—authenticity, not invention— creates the best comedy and the most effective speeches on stage and off.

I got more out of it than the audience did. I realized I'd been living in denial—not wanting to admit that I had been released from the team. I discovered that it was better for me to tell people what happened than to try to hide it; they would find out anyway, and what they heard from others might be exaggerated or even untrue. Facing my fear actually healed me from holding on to my feelings of worthlessness. I just expressed my real feelings, told my true story, on stage, and the kids found it inspirational. I brought a character (myself) to life on stage, and that character moved the audience, giving me an incredible high.

This started my love affair with speaking. Never in my wildest dreams could I have imagined that I could love to speak and be good at it. The memory of that three-minute speech in front of my small science class had convinced me that I couldn't speak. Sharing my story with these students proved I could be an effective speaker.

I began to discover other talents I'd never known I had or had given up. My first and oldest talent—art—resurfaced. Baseball had taken me in a whole different direction, but life led me right back to art, starting with the art of speaking and leading to so much more.

You, too, can discover talents you've never recognized before or re-discover talents that you've put aside. Everything you do in life is a risk. Why not take a risk on the things you really love to do? Truth be told, I still get extremely nervous before every speaking event, but I wouldn't give it up.

Here is my takeaway: Nothing will ever change to make your life what you want it to be without action on your part. Your world will never change to what you want until you deal with the root issue, which is your own insecurities, denial, and fears, as well as the pain that you've experienced.

When you accept that reality and say so, at least to yourself, I can only imagine the roar that will be set free after being caged for so long inside your heart. What kind of power will be unleashed? What sort of gifts and talents will come out of you? Only you can find out.

It's okay to admit when you're afraid; just don't allow fear to take over. I find admitting fear to myself makes dealing with pressure easier.

Then I ask, "What world do you want to build around the character?"

I then build that character and the life I want him to lead in my head. From there it's only a few more steps to bringing that character into reality.

TAKE TWO—Conquering

"Living a Limitless life is living with a roar, a fire in your heart, and showing no mercy when it comes to beating back obstacles in life."

"The world isn't all sunshine and rainbows. It's a very rough and a mean place, and no matter how tough you are, it will beat you to your knees and keep you there permanently if you let it. You, me, or nobody is never going to hit as hard as life. But it isn't about how hard you hit. It's about how hard you can get hit and keep moving forward. How much you can take and keep moving forward. If you know what you're worth, then go out and get what you're worth. But you got to be willing to take the hit."
—from the movie *Rocky Balboa*

"Life sometimes feels like you've been punched in the gut, and the only way to know what you're really made of is to get back up and finish the fight."

While mourning my brother's death, I was faced with many selfish feelings. I'd lived most of my life with this aggressive attitude. I needed an outlet. I needed to vent all my anger and face all my inner demons. I needed more than just baseball. I needed to be broken. I needed boxing as a way to vent and channel my pain.

Boxing is one of the toughest sports. It challenges every bit of your being, from the physical to the mental to the emotional.

I'd trained for about six weeks before I was put in the ring for my first, three-minute sparring session with a much younger kid who had an undefeated record. He fought with a Mayweather style, which means holding the left elbow high on the side and using the shoulder roll for defense.

Even though I wanted this fight, I was afraid. I was about to experience a beating from a more experienced fighter. I knew he was much faster because I had already seen him spar with another fighter before me. I was intimidated by his well-conditioned body and the great footwork and hand speed he displayed.

I got off to a good start, but after about thirty seconds, my legs started to give out on me. I knew I was in trouble. I tried to catch my wind and dropped my hands while taking one too many shots to the head. I was glad when the round was over.

For the next two weeks, I worked on conditioning and strengthening my legs to prepare for another sparring session. My goal: to be ready to fight at the beginning of the year at the Golden Gloves. My manager warned me that training was going to get really tough, and that he was going to push me harder.

After two weeks, we traveled to another gym to spar with other fighters. I was matched with a two-time Golden Gloves champion.

Mind you, this was only my second fight, and I was competing against trained fighters. Putting me in the ring with an undisciplined and more experienced fighter was outright wrong.

I already felt sick and weak but hoped the adrenalin would help me snap out of it. Biggest rookie mistake ever! Within the first minute of the fight I was exchanging jabs, frustrating the other fighter. He came with a low blow to the kidney then sent me a secondary low blow to the genitals, taking me out for a good two minutes. I was shaken up; everything was blurry.

I felt humiliated. No one may have heard me fart, but I did. At that moment, my image of myself was very low. Every bit of my manhood was challenged; everything about being a man was right in my face. There was no way that I was going to quit and give up on the little dignity I had left.

This is what I meant about being broken. In this moment I faced every inner self-conscious demon that made me feel insecure.

Limitless

Every negative perception or opinion of myself knocked at my front door.

THE NATURE OF THE BEAST

I thought to myself, *Is this what coach was talking about? Is this what he meant about how it was going to get tough?* So, in my mind, I said, *Oh well, I've got to keep going.*

This is the nature of the beast. When you are channeling violent anger and passion, you get all revved up in the midst of your fears.

I was getting pounded on, all the while dropping my hands, thinking he was going to hit me with another low blow. It was all a set up. He had his own strategy, and it was dirty.

After viewing the video, I realized this kid was a dirty fighter. I hadn't known the telltale signs or what a dirty fighter looked like until that fight. In that very moment, I began to reflect on how many cheap shots I've taken and the low blows I've received that had devalued me and my manhood.

But like my coach said, "In the ring and in the fight, you've got to keep going. It's going to be hard, and at times you're going to wish the fight would just hurry up and end. That, my friend, is the nature of the beast."

I don't mean that you've got to fight to find yourself. However, boxing gives you a visual and physical application of life.

What did I learn from this fight? Was it possible to come back with a victory after a humiliating defeat? The answer is, "Yes." I learned to be better at life. I learned that I would fail, that I would get beaten down, that I would have to accept defeat, but that I had to keep going.

I had to sit back and learn from my mistakes what exactly I needed to work on — what strategies I could develop to cover as many angles as possible, so that the next time I would have a victory or, at least not be so easily defeated. This applies to being a fighter in the ring with a dirty fighter or a fighter in the business world where folks will take advantage of you. They will lie through their teeth and leave you beaten down. They'll have a strategy, and it may be a dirty one. You have to stay alert, but, no matter what, you have to go back in the ring to finish the fight.

"The toughest fight you will ever face is letting go of the past."

STRATEGY

What would my strategy be going forward from that humiliating loss? I had to first face my defeat and let go—stop dwelling on the way he beat me, the way he humiliated me. But I was angry, and I wanted revenge.

Doesn't that sound like life? I have wanted revenge on so many things, so many aspects of my life, so many people who left me broken and used up.

But like Muhammad Ali, a true fighter who always believed that he was "the greatest," you have to keep speaking to that desire for revenge. You have to face the punches in life and persistently get back up. Whoever does this will eventually end up stronger and more inspiring to others.

The strategies Ali learned to use and the courage he had to face not only opponents in the ring, but also the world outside the ring, made him great. He took a stand and stood by his guns.

The book *Entering and Leaving Crisis* by
Edwin L. Cole teaches us that how you leave
one relationship will determine how you
enter the next. What you create in your mind
will attract exactly what you envision. There-
fore, creating an image in your mind of the
negative aspects of past experiences can have
a lasting — and negative — effect on your entire
life.

So I had to review the way I was thinking, because I was dwelling on my defeat. If I
built on the foundation of defeat, I was setting
myself up for another defeat. Repeating the
same strategy would be foolish and produce
the same outcome. Even if I lost again with a
new strategy, at least I'd know that I'd made
some progress and put up a better fight. That
I could live with.

In *The Godfather*, Al Pacino played the
part of Don Michael Corleone, mentoring
his nephew Vincent, played by Andy Garcia.
Vincent had an extremely bad temper. Don
Corleone made two major points about how
temper will keep any man or woman from

success. He told Vincent that his temper clouded his reasoning and he should never hate his enemies, because hate would affect his judgment.

After five years of trying to channel all my anger in the pursuit of my dreams, I realized just how much my hate toward my enemies affected my judgment—how much it held me back, even to the point of impacting my financial status.

I did nothing with a book I'd written, all because I was too angry at the people who'd injured me and the low blows that I'd taken. All that time, I could have instead been putting into play a new strategy to create success.

Have you ever felt as if you were robbed of something but you didn't know what? Like you were just mad at the world for no apparent reason? That was me—mad all the time.

I spent five years trying to overcome my own lack of forgiveness and hatred. We lose so much time buried in anger and resentment; we rob ourselves of all that time and energy while putting everything except anger on hold. This cycle of inaction and anger affects us productively, financially, and relationally.

Getting hit—getting hurt—is not defeat, but how you handle the punches determines your outlook on life. How you deal with your challenges defines you. I've learned to allow my failures to strengthen my discipline, to help me become an efficient fighter.

My coming into the world was easy, though Mom would beg to differ, but learning to live in the world was the challenge.

My heart goes out to all those living with a disability, because you have inspired me to take advantage of my privileges. My sister Jessica inspired me. My brother Juan inspired me. Those of you who live successfully even with limitations have taught me to stop whining and having pity parties.

"Feeling caged is the most miserable state of mind to be in. It hurts your soul."

I won't look at those five years of my life as wasted or ruined years. Instead, I choose to view that time as a recovery period. When you work out, you get the best results if you let your body recover in order to be healthy, refreshed, and stronger.

Life works the same way. Knowing when to step back and take a break in order to clear your mind helps you be healthy, refreshed, and stronger.

"There is a part of an artist that dies, then discovers bigger creations within himself, abilities he wouldn't have known he had without having suffered. Once he discovers the art of his skill, all he can do is sharpen that skill."

Men feel a need to be conquerors, and conquerors who have engaged in battles and had many victories inspire us. Conquerors attract opportunities. A conqueror increases his value with victory, becoming more attractive. People change their perceptions of him, which leads to opportunities. The stronger a man becomes, the more his opportunities expand.

The key element is self-control.

SELF CONTROL

Roaming like a wild animal, I was untamed, unable to make sense of life. I couldn't maintain relationships, and I couldn't control my rage or my tongue, which left marks forever on the hearts of many. I'd forgotten what it was like to be a king of the jungle. I'd forgotten what it was like to roam free, to be vulnerable but unafraid of being hurt.

Lions that walk in authority have a presence that paralyzes their prey, giving them the advantage when it comes to taking out the enemy. In our lives, confidence gives us the ability to execute wisely and gently when needed, to have self-control, and to make better decisions so that anger will not cloud our minds in the midst of confrontation.

Confidence paralyzes our prey to give us the advantage and to make successful connections where we need them in our lives. It is true in relationships, in business, and in other areas of our personal lives. Cockiness is counterfeit confidence. Confidence does not abuse its authority. Confidence always complements.

Facing danger, standing on dangerous ground, brings the battles within our hearts to the surface. Our strengths and weaknesses will be revealed. So it's necessary to step on to dangerous ground, to deal with confrontation and pressure, because then the things that we battle in our hearts will surface, giving us the opportunity to conquer.

THE JUNGLE

Getting punched in the gut is just a hit, not the end. At one point in my life, I became depressed. I felt I would never be any good to anyone. I feared that I would ruin my next relationship as a result of my past struggles or insecurities. I believed that, in spite of seeking to find a way out of messes, I would just create more.

I like to use the metaphor of a lion in a cage, in which the cage symbolizes my heart—and maybe your heart, too. That cage is filled with resentment, hate, guilt, shame, and need for revenge. Because I had been in that cage for so long, my mentor, or zoologist, took me back to the jungle and opened the cage, so I could return to being the ruler of the jungle. But because this lion had been institutional-ized for so long away from the wild, I strug-gled to leave the cage. Like a prisoner who has to re-learn how to survive in the world, I feared not making it in the wild.

Depressed people feel there is no place in this world for them to succeed. They feel like they are no longer part of society. They fear that they will never be good enough. They believe they have no purpose except to be locked up in that ridiculous cage, in solitary confinement. The world is too much for them.

The emotions we experience in the cage can keep us from taking a step out. Ask yourself: What kind of solitary confinement are you putting yourself in because you're too afraid to pursue your dreams? Are you afraid of taking that risk, worrying that what you have to offer may not be valuable enough?

But you can't run a car without the negative charge to complement the positive one, and a story without a negative never inspires us to reach for the positive. We need the down times to get to the good times. Without the down times to conquer, the victory means little. During my journey of self-discovery, I've learned that I am my own worst enemy. I am the villain of my own destiny, and the only one who can keep me from pursuing that destiny is me.

Men and women both can build their confidence while in the jungle. They can unleash their power to roar again. They can unleash their ability to rule over themselves in a positive way. They can unleash themselves from being the prey to become a king or a queen of the jungle, a conqueror! They can free themselves from the cage of the past. In the jungle, a person can renew the mind and bring change to the heart. An untamed lion is a dangerous beast.

The great and influential Arnold Schwarzenegger plays the part of Conan in of one of my favorite movies, *Conan the Barbarian*. Conan escapes his destiny after being sold into slavery. He becomes a gladiator, discovering his ability and his self-worth in battle. His confidence becomes stronger. His master ultimately sets him free because he realizes Conan has been locked up too long. Conan roams alone, conquering his enemies, but he is not all beast. He favors the weak and saves other fighters when he can. They beg to follow him.

"I will live for you and die for you," they say, because they want to be a part of a conquering barbarian.

An unleashed man is a man who knows his purpose. Humans were made to be unleashed, to roam free. A man with a healed heart can roam free and still exercise self-control. Rather than being controlled by other people or by his negative emotions, he controls his own life and lives it to the fullest. By conquering my heart, I was able to influence and impact others. Just like Conan, each of us can discover the influence we have on others when we recognize our own self-worth.

What is in the cage that is keeping you captive? Look outside the cage and claim your success!

TAKE THREE—The Nasty Change-up

"Life will throw you fastballs and curveballs, but nothing is as deceptive as the change-up. The key to hitting that pitch is patience and trust in self."

I will never forget when baseball came into my life and helped form the one principle that guides everything I do.

When my family relocated from Mexico to the United States, I was four years old. I, along with my two younger brothers, knew no English. The street I grew up on in my early years was called Lover's Lane. How ironic that all my life I have been a seeker of love, passionate about creating and expressing that love in many ways through art.

Baseball was a form of art, and I spent years trying to master it. I made every effort to make it to the "Show," meaning the Major League.

The odds were against me when I was growing up. Age, time, and opinions have always been against me. I started playing baseball at a late age—seven years old—and never learned the basic principles to hitting a baseball.

I had not yet learned the one basic principle on which to build my life. I had not yet figured out that the foundation of success is confidence.

In my first experience at the plate, I was so focused on not getting hit by the ball, I watched every baseball go by, never taking a swing because I was more prepared to not get hit than I was prepared to hit the ball.

My coach at the time said, "Pablo, I don't care where the baseball is, just swing the bat, son! I don't care if the ball is on the ground, high, or far to the outside, or even if it's coming right at you! Just swing the bat!"

From my years in baseball, I've learned something that I've carried into how I live my life now: If I don't ever swing the bat, I'll never know if I can hit the ball. The fear I had of being hit by the ball kept me from swinging, and if I did swing, I hesitated to follow through.

The same applies to you. Whatever dreams you want to fulfill or fears you want to overcome, you've got to be willing to step up to the plate and swing the bat with all you've got until you finally connect.

Although I was a strikeout king growing up, after consistently swinging and swinging and swinging, I finally overcame my fears and eventually started connecting. And not only was I connecting, I was hitting the ball hard! The truth is, I didn't realize how hard I could hit until I actually connected.

No matter who is watching you or what perceptions you have of yourself, sometimes you just have to swing hard. As long as you know you gave it your best, nothing else matters. At the end of the day, you're the only one who is victimized by your own fears. I can't count how many people I've talked to who never pursued their dreams because they feared failure. So they settled for mediocrity. That's no way to live a life.

"Never let the fear of striking out keep you
from coming up to bat."
—Babe Ruth

There are two boxes in baseball that I
dreaded being in: the dugout when I wasn't
worth being put in the game, and the batter's
box, where four possible things happened: I
either struck out and went back to the dugout;
I advanced to first if I got a hit; I got a free
pass to advance because the pitcher walked
me; or, I was hit by the ball. I was the one who
held the bat and the skill in my hands, and it
was up to me to get out of the box. If I allowed
others to put me in that box, I would never
advance or accomplish my dreams.

I went off to three disappointing college
baseball tryouts and never made the teams.
I was so nervous and afraid. All the other
players looked way too good. Proving to the
coach that I was the better fit was the biggest
challenge of my career. Fear crippled my
inability to play at the level of confidence I had
when I played defense. That was my greatest

asset, but like my coach said, "Just swing the bat, son. Eventually you will hit it!"

So I kept trying out until I reached the confidence level I needed to show that I could get the job done.

On the fourth tryout I finally made it on with Calhoun State in Alabama. I was excited not only to make it on the squad but also to receive a full scholarship.

I couldn't believe what was happening. Every part of my life—from building character to facing and conquering the change-ups— finally came together. I was hitting.

I have applied that one basic principle— just swing—to many areas of life. I've used it to start a business, go for more tryouts, audition for my next acting role, and create my own production company so I could create my own opportunities in film.

During my college baseball career, I went from one college to the next, losing two full scholarships as a result of my uncontrolled anger. I struggled to trust and submit to authority because of the abusive authority I had experienced in the past.

Soon, I was no longer playing organized ball. That was the hardest bench I have ever sat on. All the opportunities I had been given were a result of my hard work, but I just couldn't maintain the role.

My father always said, "It's easy to get into a relationship, but learning to live with the person is another matter altogether." Opportunities will always come along, but I needed to learn how to live and maintain my life in that world. I had to learn to deal with people and to live with them in whatever capacity was set before me.

Not long after I lost my second scholarship, I found myself with very little money, in the dead of winter, living out of my parents' Suburban, trying to make it on to the next team.

Unfortunately when coaches called the colleges where I'd played previously, the reports they got ruined my chances for those opportunities. My anger had finally caught up to what I was most passionate about. I had burned all my bridges. I was so discouraged I decided to take a break from even trying to get back into baseball.

Two years later, I was introduced to the book *You Can If You Think You Can*, by Norman Vincent Peale. At first, I wasn't interested in reading a book. I hated reading and considered it a waste of time, but in desperation and curiosity, I read.

To my amazement, I discovered that every word I'd ever spoken affected my thoughts and formed fears and doubts in my life on top of what had already been destroyed by my past behavior. I immersed myself in this book because it taught me the power of words. I became a lover of words and learned to use their power to create what I wanted.

Muhammad Ali constantly said, "I am the greatest!" and that's exactly what he became. Mike Tyson's manager, Cus D'Amato, helped Tyson change his perspective of himself from negative to positive by way of words, and thus constructed a more confident "Iron Mike" Tyson.

So I began to change the way I thought and the way I viewed myself.

Physically practicing ball was one thing. Believing in myself was another. Every time I was up to bat, out of fear, I'd focused more on striking out than on hitting the ball.

Then I started to think, *if I think I can, then I can*. I had to prepare my mind and refocus all my energy on my goal: not only to hit the ball, but also to be consistent. After years of failing because of lack of preparation, I was going to be prepared this time.

"Don't get caught flat-footed when opportunities come your way."

I then started telling myself that I would crush the ball, even if I struck out. I kept saying it even as I walked back to the dugout.

During my first pro game, I struck out the first time I was at bat. On the second at bat, I was hit right on the back of my hamstring.

I tried not to rub it, for that is forbidden in baseball. So while I limped and grimaced all the way to first base, I repeated, "I will crush the ball," while my teammates laughed at me and said, "Don't rub it! Don't rub it!"

Oh! How badly I wanted to. I kept repeating, "I will crush the ball" while in the dugout, in the outfield, in my workouts. That became my mantra.

On my third at bat, as the pitcher made his release, my mind focused on the words, "I will crush the ball," until the words themselves became a creation in my mind to the point it became an instinct.

To my surprise, I actually crushed it into the right field line. I was so in shock that all I could do was run for my life, while all these mixed emotions coursed through my body. I ran as I had never run in my entire life. As I rounded first on my way to second, I turned to look at my third base coach and saw him waving me to keep coming. And, as I was halfway from second to third base, he was already telling me to get down, which meant I had to slide into the bag.

I became worried at that point, because I thought I was going to get gunned down and called out. I slid in too early, trying to get there. My adrenalin must have been on fire; it felt like I slid for a long time, almost past the bag.

I'd hit a triple in the pros at my third at bat, and the fans went wild! It was the best feeling in the world. That became the mark and the turning point of my life.

The power of words created in my mind what I wanted most in my heart, and it inevitably became a reality. The rest was history. I had just proven to myself the power of self-motivation, and, to top it off, in my rookie year, we won the championship series. My self-confidence grew, and I learned to deal with pressure on a whole new scale.

In life, pressures in relationships and in business fill people with emotions. To deal with these emotions, I developed a philosophy based on simple principles I learned through baseball.

First, I may not know about statistics, but one thing I do know is pressure. When it comes down to it, money doesn't matter when life's issues hit the roof. Just ask the men and women who were wealthy and made one bad decision that sent them off to a cage (prison).

How do you handle pressure when you're in the playoffs? How does an athlete handle the pitcher and the fans and traveling to places he's never been? What sort of jungle have we come to? What kind of beast is ahead of us? The pressure is on!

The ability to deal with pressure is what separates the weak from the strong, the losers from the champions. It's what separates players from high school to college to the pros. Dealing with pressure takes guts and confidence.

The ability to deal with pressure will determine the next stage of your life and take you to places you've never been. Every stage of life brings ugly tricks to get you off track.

Life will throw you fastballs and curveballs, but nothing is as deceptive as the change-up.

A change-up is a pitch that at first looks like a fastball, but right when it gets in front of you, it sort of just drops and seems to go backward. The key to hitting it is patience and trust in yourself.

Pitchers have thrown fastballs to my head to mess with me psychologically. A pitcher's mission is to strike out the batter, and he will do everything he can to set you up to fail. He will try to use fear to slow down your reaction time. Then he'll throw you a curveball to get you to freeze and strike out. Or he'll throw a change-up, making you chase the pitch and strike out. That, in my opinion, is the nastiest pitch.

The change-up reminds me of a good liar. When a pitcher throws a fastball, he throws it with all he's got, releasing the ball with a fast arm motion. But on the change-up the pitcher holds the ball a little bit differently, coming on with the exact same fast arm motion. A change-up comes ten to thirty miles an hour slower, depending on how good the pitcher is at throwing one, and only disciplined hitters can compete against a good pitcher.

Over and over, I have struggled hitting this pitch, and I finally heeded the words of Albert Einstein: "Insanity is doing the same thing over and over again and expecting different results." I needed to change my habits.

So I turned to a basic training tool, one I'd never used because I found it boring: the tee. The tee, in baseball, is an apparatus on which a ball sits. By allowing you to hit baseballs from a stopped position, it teaches and builds physical body mechanics and creates a patient, disciplined hitter. This simple tool trains for consistent hitting and power. Using the tee helps you become a controlled hitter who sits back and waits to determine the type of pitch the pitcher is throwing and reacts appropriately.

Ichiro Suzuki was the master of the tee, and that is why, in a world that often looks at the size of an athlete rather than his heart, he was the best 165-pound, consistent hitter in the Major League.

In life, we chase too many things that look good and promising, like that juicy fast-ball that I so love to hit! Instead, I find myself chasing that nasty change-up and striking out. Had I learned earlier in my life the importance of the tee, I would have made that a priority in my life as a baseball player.

And if I'd learned to sit back and wait to see what that business deal really was, I could have avoided striking out and losing so much money. If I'd had more patience and disci-pline, I wouldn't have gotten into that rela-tionship too fast, costing both of us not only money, but also precious time.

Thanks to the philosophy of the tee, I've learned to trust my hands and the abilities I have to offer. I am valuable to the team no matter what part of the lineup I'm in, or whether in high school, college, or the pros. If I do my part, I trust that I will be recognized.

Everyone has value, and if you can sit back patiently, you begin to see how much you have to offer. The famous Babe Ruth said, "The way a team plays as a whole determines its success. You may have the greatest bunch of individual stars in the world, but if they don't play together, the club won't be worth a dime."

"Doubt is poisonous to the mind. It paralyzes your creativity and your ability to believe in yourself."

You are just as valuable as the next guy or gal! Perception can be our worst enemy. There were three things that I struggled with throughout my life: my perception of myself, others' perception of me, and the real me. This created so many doubts, paralyzing me when it came to using the abilities I had to excel in life. I focused too much on those first two issues rather than on my mission.

I played the outfield defensively, and my mission was to catch that ball. Defense was my biggest strength in baseball. Offense was my weakness in sports. However, the defensiveness that worked on the field got me nowhere in life. As I became better in my offense as a hitter, my confidence in myself grew outside of baseball, in my social life and in business networking. Confidence in offense, in putting myself out there, helped my ability to approach people.

Playing in the outfield, my mission was to catch that ball. When a batter hit the ball, all sounds, perceptions, and doubts went out the window. In my perspective, all I saw was that ball. When it was hit, it was mine. I wanted it and went after it. I was so in the zone that, at times, I'd be headed for the fence and not even know it.

My teammates would yell, "Wall, wall, wall!" to let me know I was nearing the fence, but I never actually heard them, because I was so focused on catching that ball. Most of the time I'd catch that ball within inches of running into the wall, but sometimes, I'd hit it. And I mean hard, so much so that people across the stadium could hear a loud bang from my head hitting the wall.

Walls will be there in life, and you'll encounter people who have failed in their own lives. They'll be like the players who yell, "Wall, wall, wall," but instead of warning you, they can create a distraction. Fear can slow you down from your mission and your goals.

If you look at why others fail, you'll discover that they had no guts, no strategy, no stability, and they didn't have their priorities in order. My defense was my strength up to a point, and I focused on that till my offense leveled up to my defense.

What are your strengths? What are your walls?

Consistency is the key, and if you're consistent, you'll progress in whatever you do. Know your mission. Practice the tee to produce consistent success.

What are the bad habits you need to change, and the basics that you need to build on? What is the tee—the basic tool you need to work on—in your life? What is your mission?

See your vision and go after it! Change your strategy so you're not fooled by the change-up.

"If you're consistent, then you will progress in whatever you do."

WHAT ARE YOUR FEARS?

Ask yourself what your fears are, specifically. Are you afraid to swing the bat?

Are you afraid of failure when doing business face-to-face? Do relationships scare you when they get really intimate? Do the opinions of others frighten you?

You see, once I learned to focus on the baseball, I noticed that I'd learned to block out all the booing, the critical words, the negative opinions, the gossip, and the jealousy.

"Find your focus, and you will find your way through the chaos."

CUT—Epilogue

"When you place your destiny in the hands of someone else, you risk never reaching what you're destined to be."

If you've made it this far to the Cut, whatever area of life you're in, you know that life is filled with circumstances that will throw you a change-up. The passing of my brother stretched my heart so big, leaving so much empty space to fill, I was not sure how I'd ever get beyond the loss.

In all my pondering, I realized there are two things that you can do in life when your heart has been stretched: you can either fill it up with bitterness or you can fill it up with love. Which you choose will determine whether you live a miserable life or a very rich, full, and happy one.

Over the years, I believed in the people I'd submitted my life to and trusted that they would build me up and push me into achievement just like Cus did with Mike Tyson. But instead, those I gave my life to put me through a nightmare.

In our lives we'll trust teachers, coaches, and leaders who will help elevate us into our destinies. But, keep in mind and beware, not all are there to help you succeed. Some may only take advantage of you. Be careful into whose hands you place your destiny, because they can either increase your value or decrease it.

I began to discover talents later in life. I had big ambitions that were much bigger than me and sometimes too overwhelming for my heart to handle. The loss of my brother was a turning point of my life. It opened my heart to the point that it became big enough to wrap around the ambitions that were bigger than myself. So, I went after those ambitions.

If I'd just sat around and had a pity party, my life's dreams would have been no more than that: dreams. I don't like to use the word "handicapped" to describe my brother, but he fought through his limits. If I failed to pursue my dreams, the legacy he left behind would have gone to waste. I owed it to myself and to him to embark on the journey,

Although I've learned to take negatives and channel them into positives, this was the greatest challenge in my life. In the end, you see me as the finished product of meeting these challenges. But there will be more challenges, and I will have to face up to them in a positive rather than self-destructive manner.

I wish you the best in your personal journey and hope that you can now see how beautiful life can be in the creation of your own art. As you transition from old ways of thinking into the new, remember the three basic takeaways: Building Character, Conquering Fears, and getting past that Nasty Change-Up.

"If you're a fighter, truly a fighter, then you get back up. You fight again."
—from the film *Manny* narrated by Liam Neeson

Pablo De Leon

"Don't think you are. Know you are."
—from the film *Matrix*

I wake; I stare and ponder. I see in the distance my destiny. In my mind, it seems so close, yet so far from reach. My enemies lay before me—and I don't mean people. They are doubt, discouragement, and, the worst of all, fear.

Fear is what angers me the most. I've come to hate fear so much I can't help but face it. I will no longer let it rule my life or allow others to place it into my heart. I am the creator of my own destiny.

You are *Limitless*!

ACKNOWLEDGEMENTS

Thanks to family and friends who supported
me along the journey:

Dad, Mom, brothers, and sisters for sticking
together and staying strong.

Jon Reyna, for listening to my madness.

Vanessa Vargas, for keeping it real!

Melissa Rios, for always challenging me.

David Nieves, for being you. Motivator!
You're a great friend!

Team Grind:
Director: Reggie Titus
Producer: Casey G. Smith
Music Supervisor: Adrien Johnson
Editor: Ramsey Rodriguez

. . . for building me up, keeping me focused
and grounded.

Pablo De Leon Enterprise
www.pablo-deleon.com

CPSIA information can be obtained at www.ICGtesting.com
Printed in the USA
BVOW02*1857011015

420627BV00003B/6/P